**Elijah Muhammad—
Original Man Know Thyself**

FIRST EDITION

ELIJAH MUHAMMAD—ORIGINAL MAN KNOW THYSELF

A Pedagogy for Black Liberation

Abul Pitre, PhD
San Francisco State University

Bassim Hamadeh, CEO and Publisher
Seidy Cruz, Senior Field Acquisitions Editor
Anne Jones, Project Editor
Susana Christie, Senior Developmental Editor
Alia Bales, Production Editor
Asfa Arshi, Graphic Design Assistant
Trey Soto, Licensing Specialist
Natalie Piccotti, Director of Marketing
Kassie Graves, Senior Vice President of Editorial
Jamie Giganti, Director of Academic Publishing

Copyright © 2022 by Cognella, Inc. All rights reserved. No part of this publication may be reprinted, reproduced, transmitted, or utilized in any form or by any electronic, mechanical, or other means, now known or hereafter invented, including photocopying, microfilming, and recording, or in any information retrieval system without the written permission of Cognella, Inc. For inquiries regarding permissions, translations, foreign rights, audio rights, and any other forms of reproduction, please contact the Cognella Licensing Department at rights@cognella.com.

Trademark Notice: Product or corporate names may be trademarks or registered trademarks and are used only for identification and explanation without intent to infringe.

Cover image copyright © 2018 Depositphotos/fckncg.

Printed in the United States of America.

This book is dedicated in memory of Joseph and Beatrice Holden, Dr. James Conyers, Joshua Pitre, Marion White, and Clifton Lemelle. You are still present in spirit.

Contents

Preface ix

Elijah Muhammad xvii

A Pedagogy of Liberation xxiii

SELECTION 1. Re-Educate the Blackman 1

SELECTION 2. Who Is That Mystery God? 7

SELECTION 3. Know Thyself 13

SELECTION 4. Get Knowledge to Benefit Self 19

SELECTION 5. If the Civilized Man Fails to Perform His Duty, What Must Be Done? 27

SELECTION 6. Beautiful Appearance and Long Life 31

SELECTION 7. The Bad Food and Drinks You Should Shun 37

SELECTION 8. Savagery of America 41

SELECTION 9. He (Allah) Makes All Things New 45

About the Author 51

Preface

The crisis of educating Black students continues to be a concern for scholars and policy makers (Banks, 2019; Howard, 2020; Ladson-Billings, 1995; McLaren, 2015; Pitre, 2019; Spring, 2016). At the center of this concern is closing the achievement gap between Black and White students. As a result, educators are being required to focus on raising test scores.

Testing has become a weapon used to label Black students as being deficient. Under the disguise of improving the educational outcomes of Black students, policy makers have caused schools to become places that resemble prisons. Black bodies are policed, and their intelligence is subtly brought into question (Ladson-Billings, 2011).

James Baldwin (2019) eloquently wrote that Black people are viewed through the lens of criminality, and he discloses White fear of an educated Black populace. Testing is a throwback to the eugenics movement and is one of the ways those ruling society can ensure Blacks never discover their creative genius. The eugenics movement was started in Europe and entailed labeling people as being genetically inferior. Through intelligence tests, eugenicists claimed Blacks were an inferior race (Watkins, 2001).

When Amanda Gorman spoke at the Biden and Harris inauguration, the world marveled. However, just a few weeks afterward, she was "followed home and accosted by a security guard who allegedly claimed she looked suspicious" (Busby, 2021). This type of racial profiling is common.

Another injustice is occurring throughout public schools in America. Black children's gifts and talents are suffocated because schools are graded on test scores. The focus on testing has muted Black students while those in high places get rich off of educational gimmicks that they claim will improve test scores. Education has become like McDonald's—teaching has been reduced to prepackaged material that teachers are forced to use (McLaren, 2015). Pacing guides dominate in some Black schools and reflect a pedagogy centered around rote learning and memorization. Martin Haberman (1991) described this as a pedagogy of poverty.

Under the disguise of equity and social justice, there is a hidden agenda that domesticates the masses of students (Freire, 2000; Gatto, 2017). The ideology that schools should prepare workers undergirds educational policy and is based on human capitalist economics (Spring, 2011). The preparation of workers aligns with the needs of the super-rich, who are the slave makers of the poor (Muhammad, 1993).

Weaponized education becomes the tool to domesticate people. Woodson (1999 [1933]) pointed out that you don't need to force people to the back door, because you can educate them in a way that if there is no back door, they will make one. Chomsky (1988) wrote that the Trilateral Commission's goal of education was to indoctrinate the young, "for imposing obedience, for blocking the possibility of independent thought, and they play an institutional role in a system of control and coercion" (p. 681).

This process of educating for control is best seen in the Black experience in America. The institution of slavery resulted in the original brainwashing. Blacks were stripped of their language, culture, and religion (Hine et al., 2009).

In the pamphlet "The Making of a Slave," by Willie Lynch, the human capitalist ideology is disclosed: "Hence both the horse and the nigger must be broken that is break them from one form of mental life to another—keep the body and take the mind" (Hassan-El,

1999, p. 14). The 21st-century educational system operates under the same premise.

When the term *negro* was applied to Black people, it meant that slave owners had caused their mental death. Akbar (1998) wrote that devious White scholars used the term *negro* to hide the fact that it really meant *necro*. *Necro* means "dead," and through White dominance in education, the true power of Black genius was put to sleep. The best example of this is that it was once a crime for Blacks to read (Spring, 2016).

Through their critiques, critical educational scholars have addressed many of the problems facing diverse student populations (Apple, 2019; Darder et al., 2017; McLaren, 2015; Milner, 2019; Theoharis & Scanlan, 2020). They have asked questions about curriculum such as, *Who determines what is learned in school?* They have argued that those who have the power determine what is placed in the curriculum (Apple, 2019). These scholars have also explored how racial inequality permeates schools (King, 1991; Ladson-Billings, 1995; Milner, 2019).

Multicultural education scholars have disclosed how the pedagogy used in schools is Eurocentric (Banks, 2019; Nieto & Bode, 2018). They have argued that diverse perspectives should be infused into the curriculum (Banks, 2019). Moreover, they have highlighted how what is taught in schools is disconnected from the lives of non-White students (Banks, 2019; Gollnick & Chinn, 2017; Nieto & Bode, 2018; Sleeter & Grant, 2009).

Through Eurocentric education, Whites are the heroes and heroines (Asante, 1991). They are the people who produced all the good the modern world has experienced. Non-Whites should recognize that Whites are world saviors. In schools, children from oppressed groups are taught to give their allegiance to White power cloaked under symbols like the American flag.

Through the hidden curriculum, students believe that America stands for freedom and justice without realizing this has not been the lived reality for oppressed people. Pinar (2004) called this an "official story":

> The official story a nation or culture tells itself—often evident in school curriculum—hides other truths. The national story also creates the illusion of truth being on the social surface, when it is nearly axiomatic that the stories we tell ourselves mask the unacceptable truths. What we as a nation try not to remember—genocide, slavery, lynching, prison rape—structures the politics of our collective identification and imagined affiliation. (p. 38)

This official story then becomes a way of doing what Woodson (1999 [1933]) termed "mis-educating" students. This is also seen in textbooks, where the imagery reflects a Eurocentric dominance that teaches non-White students to view the world from the perspectives of those in the dominating class.

As result of Eurocentric education, students from oppressed groups are more likely to serve the interests of their oppressors (Freire, 2000). Steven Biko, a South African apartheid activist, was correct when he said that the minds of oppressed people are the most potent weapon their oppressors can have (Stubbs, 2002). While there seems to be no end to the educational dilemmas facing Black students, there are models of education that could radically transform their education. Elijah Muhammad's teachings offer an educational blueprint that could transform the education of oppressed people.

His teachings were a forerunner to critical pedagogy, critical race theory, and critical whiteness studies. The model of education that he offered produced intellectual and spiritual giants that the world continues to marvel. Elijah Muhammad—with only a fourth-grade education—was a wonder among us, producing a people that were unlike the masses. Through reeducation, he brought a whole new culture to Blacks in America.

The knowledge that he espoused awakened Black people, and it caused him to be the number-one adversary of those ruling society. His teachings raised the consciousness of Black people and sparked their desire for more knowledge of themselves.

College students influenced by his pupil, Malcolm X, demanded courses that reflected the Black experience. Their protest gave birth to Black Studies, ethnic studies, and multicultural education (Banks, 1992). The teachings of Elijah Muhammad made Black consciousness a reality. Unfortunately, his contribution to the discipline of education has been absent despite the fact that he was a progenitor of multicultural discourse (Pitre, 2015).

This volume introduces readers to nine selections, one of which comes from the *Muhammad Speaks* newspaper and the rest of which are from Elijah Muhammad's classic books, *Message to the Blackman in America*, *How to Eat to Live*, and *Our Savior Has Arrived*. Together these selections offer an example of how Elijah Muhammad's teachings offer a pedagogy of liberation. The selections are excerpted but can be read from their original source documents.

When James Cone (2010 [1970]) wrote his classic book, *A Black Theology of Liberation*, it captured the work of Elijah Muhammad. Etymologically the term pedagogy means a teacher who walks alongside a student on a journey. The teachings of Elijah Muhammad awakened his students to the teacher within, causing them to be knowledge seekers who were committed to the liberation of oppressed people.

In addition to a focus on education, this book demonstrates how the teachings of Elijah Muhammad have contributed to Africana/Black Studies. The volume also includes reflective questions that can stimulate discussion about the applications of these teachings to contemporary educational practice.

REFERENCES

Akbar, N. (1998). *Know thyself*. Mind Productions & Associates.

Apple, M. (2019). *Ideology and curriculum* (4th ed.). Routledge.

Asante, M. K. (1991). The Afrocentric idea in education. *Journal of Negro Education*, 60(2), 170–179.

Baldwin, J. (2019). A talk to teachers. In A. Pitre (Ed.), *A critical Black pedagogy reader: The brothers speak* (pp. 53–61). Rowman and Littlefield.

Banks, J. A. (1992). African American scholarship and the evolution of multicultural education. *Journal of Negro Education*, 61(3), 273-286.

Banks, J. A. (2019). *An introduction to multicultural education* (6th ed.). Pearson.

Busby, M. (2021, March 6). Amanda Gorman tells of being followed by security guard who said she looked "suspicious." *The Guardian*. https://www.theguardian.com/us-news/2021/mar/06/amanda-gorman-says-she-was-followed-by-security-guard-who-said-she-looked-suspicious

Chomsky, N. (1988). *Language and politics*. Black Rose Books.

Cone, J. (2010). *A Black theology of liberation*. Oribis Books. (Original work published 1970.)

Darder, A., Torres, R., & Baltodano, M. (Eds.). (2017). *The critical pedagogy reader* (3rd ed.). Routledge.

Freire, P. (2000). *Pedagogy of the oppressed*. Continuum.

Gatto, J. T. (2017). *Dumbing us down: The hidden curriculum of compulsory schooling*. New Society Publishers.

Gollnick, D. M., & Chinn, P. C. (2017). *Multicultural education in a pluralistic society* (10th ed.). Pearson.

Haberman, M. (1991). The pedagogy of poverty versus good teaching. *The Phi Delta Kappan*, 73(4), 290-294.

Hassan-El, K. (1999). *The Willie Lynch letter and the making of a slave*. UBUS Communication.

Hine, D., Hine, W., & Harrold, S. (2009). *African Americans: A concise history* (3rd ed.). Pearson.

Howard, T. (2020). *Why race and culture matter in schools: Closing the achievement gap in America's classrooms* (2nd ed.). Teachers College Press.

King, J. (1991). Dysconscious racism: Ideology, identity and the miseducation of teachers. *Journal of Negro Education, 60*, 133–146.

Ladson-Billings, G. (1995). But that's just good teaching! The case for culturally relevant pedagogy. *Theory into Practice, 34*(3), 59–65.

Ladson-Billings, G. (2011). Boyz to men? Teaching to restore Black boys' childhood. *Race, Ethnicity and Education, 14*(1), 7–15.

McLaren, P. (2015). *Life in schools: An introduction to critical pedagogy in the foundations of education* (6th ed.). Routledge.

Milner, R. (2019). Race to improve teacher education: Building awareness for instructional practice. *American Educator, 3*, 13–17.

Muhammad, E. (1993). *Supreme wisdom*. Final Call.

Nieto, S., & Bode, P. (2018). *Affirming diversity: The sociopolitical context of multicultural education*. Pearson.

Pinar, W. (2004). *What is curriculum theory?* Lawrence Erlbaum Associates.

Pitre, A. (2015). *Educational philosophy of Elijah Muhammad: Education for a new world* (3rd ed.). Hamilton Books.

Pitre, A. (Ed.). (2019). *A critical Black pedagogy reader: The brothers speak*. Rowman and Littlefield.

Sleeter, C., & Grant, C. (2009). *Making choices for multicultural education: Five approaches to race, class and gender* (6th ed.). Wiley.

Spring, J. H. (2011). *The politics of American education*. Routledge.

Spring, J. H. (2016). *Deculturalization and the struggle for equality: Brief history of the education of dominated cultures in the United States*. Routledge.

Stubbs, A. (Ed.). (2002). *Steve Biko—I write what I like: Selected writings*. University of Chicago Press. (Original work published 1978.)

Theoharis, G., & Scanlan, M. (2020). *Leadership for increasingly diverse schools* (2nd ed.). Routledge.

Watkins, W. (2001). *The white architects of Black education: Ideology and power in America, 1865-1954*. Teachers College Press.

Woodson, C. G. (1999). *The mis-education of the Negro*. UBUS Communication. (Original work published 1933.)

Elijah Muhammad

A Biographical Sketch

The name Elijah Muhammad is frightening to many people. As he has been portrayed in the media in the most negative way, the masses are clueless as to the many ways Elijah Muhammad's teachings have given rise to many of the new scientific and technological advancements we are currently experiencing. Throughout his lifetime he was the target of a misinformation campaign that sought to destroy the power of his teachings to raise the consciousness of Blacks in America. J. Edgar Hoover's Counterintelligence Program fabricated news articles about him, wiretapped his home, and placed agent provocateurs inside his organization to assassinate his character.

This section offers an overview of his life. As a sketch it doesn't scratch the surface of the 44 years of leadership that he provided to Blacks in America. Minister Farrakhan (2016) writes that Elijah Muhammad was a true friend to the Black man and woman because of the relevancy of his teachings in modern times.

Jabril Muhammad (1996) accurately describes the challenge of writing about Elijah Muhammad when he says that he is

> [l]oved intensely by a growing minority, hated fiercely by a decreasing majority, understood by some, misjudged by most, he is the type of man who evokes the greatest interest and stirs the deepest emotions. What he says and does forces men to think, to move,

to take a stand. He is a man about whom none can be neutral. (p. 137)

Elijah Muhammad was born Elijah Poole in rural Sandersville, Georgia, around October 7, 1897. Muhammad's early education was more spiritual than the traditional education that many today are familiar with. Elijah Muhammad only completed the fourth grade, and then, like so many Blacks during that time, he had to work in order to make sure that his family could survive.

This lack of formal education was supplemented with a strong spiritual education. Elijah's father was a Baptist minister in the area, which resulted in him having a familiarity with biblical scripture. In *The Theology of Time*, Muhammad (2006) mentioned studying the words of his father so that at some point he could debate with him the interpretation of the scriptures.

During Muhammad's lifetime, he experienced the suffering of Black people. This suffering was probably exacerbated when he witnessed firsthand the lynching of a Black man in the Sandersville area (Sahib, 1951). In his writings, Muhammad often referred to those experiences in Sandersville and the South as being proof that White people were bent on keeping Blacks from ever achieving true justice and equality.

The Great Depression and the racism of the South forced Elijah and his wife, Clara, along with their two children, to move to Detroit, Michigan, in 1923 (Muhammad, 1965). Prior to leaving the South, Elijah worked for the Southern Railroad Company and the Cherokee Brick Company (Hakim, 1997). Once in Detroit, at the urging of his relatives, he attended a meeting in September of 1931 to hear a lecture by W. D. Fard (J. Muhammad, 1996).

At first Elijah, the son of a Baptist minister, was somewhat reluctant to attend the lecture because he considered Islam to be heathenism. However, after hearing through relatives what was being taught by Mr. Fard, he decided to attend one of Fard's lectures.

> I first heard Islam in Detroit, Michigan back in the early fall of 1931. I heard that there was a man teaching Islam by the name of Mr. Wallace Fard. At that time, he mostly used the initial Mr. W.D. Fard. When I heard what was said, I wanted to meet him. Finally, I met him. When I looked at him, it just came to me that this is the son of man which the Bible prophesied will come in the last days of the world, and I couldn't get that out of me. I shook hands with him and I said to him, you are the One that the Bible prophesied will come at the end of the world under the name of the son of man and under the name of the second coming of Jesus. (Hakim, 1997, p. 36)

For the next three years and four months, Elijah Poole was under the tutelage of Mr. Fard. Jabril Muhammad (1996) elaborated on what occurred during that time:

> They would often sit from the early part of the night and continue to sunrise and beyond. He constantly taught him things of Islam, of that which was before, and of what was to come. They were practically inseparable. There were times when Mr. Fard carried Elijah just outside of town in his Chevy Coupe. They would sit many hours while he taught his pupil many facts about the universe. It is very interesting to see that the scientists of this world bear witness to many of the scientific facts the Honorable Elijah Muhammad was taught and made known years ago—before they knew or confirmed them for themselves. (p. 152)

Fard was depositing himself in Elijah Poole to give birth to Elijah Muhammad. After spending three years and four months learning from Fard, the fourth-grade student became a master teacher, ready to disclose knowledge that the entire world had never heard before. Muhammad shattered traditionalist religious perspectives when he said God was a human being, and moreover, a Black man. He disclosed a history of the Black man that predated the sun, moon, and stars (Muhammad, 1974).

Prior to meeting Fard, Elijah was a heavy drinker. In today's world, he perhaps would be likened to gangster rappers and a consumer of the popular drug marijuana. Found in a drunken state and not conscious of how the White man's world led to spiritual death, his life was transformed. Elijah Poole died and he took on a new life as a result of his *new education*. He became Elijah Muhammad, the Messenger of Allah.

When Fard departed, one of the first acts that took place under the leadership of Elijah Muhammad was the establishment of a university. Elijah Muhammad was arrested for founding the university:

> Then I committed myself to the jail in Detroit after learning that the Michigan State Board of Education had arrested the Muslim Teachers of the school of Islam and the secretary of the temple on false charges of contributing to the delinquency of minors. This false charge was dropped, and the teachers were freed. I was at that time given 6 months probation to put our Muslim children back in the public schools under Christian teachers. This I did not do and I moved in September of that same year to Chicago. (Hakim, 1997, p. 35)

Muhammad's arrest for developing a school to educate Black children demonstrated the importance of education. After Fard's departure there were those in the Nation of Islam who sought to take the life of Elijah Muhammad because he declared that he was the Messenger of Allah. To avoid those who were seeking to take his life he traveled to the East Coast, where he stayed with different families under an alias.

Prior to Fard's departure, he assigned Elijah Muhammad 104 books to read. It was during Muhammad's travels on the East Coast that he came to the realization that those books were housed in the Congressional Library (Hakim, 1997). These 104 books gave him insights into the experiences that he would encounter in establishing the Nation of Islam in America.

In 1942, he was arrested under the false charge of draft evasion. He spent nearly five years in jail because the federal government did not want him teaching while America was fighting in World War II. After his release from prison he began to solidify the Nation of Islam. His leadership of the Nation of Islam led to the establishment of a wide range of businesses, an educational system, land acquisition, and international trade. His teachings transformed the lives of countless people. Persons like Malcolm X, Muhammad Ali, and Minister Louis Farrakhan became world leaders who raised the consciousness of people from diverse walks of life.

From 1934 to 1975, the unlettered man from rural Sandersville, Georgia, developed an entire nation based on an educational program that reshaped Black thought. Toure Muhammad (1996) wrote of his accomplishments:

> The Most Honorable Elijah Muhammad, a man raised from the mud, built a well disciplined, organized body of Black men and women whose unity and hard work developed an $80 million dollar empire and forever changed the mentality of Black people. He established an organization that provided food, clothing, and shelter for Black Americans. (p. 15)

The teachings of Elijah Muhammad raised the consciousness of Black people throughout the world. Moreover, he provided a blueprint for the liberation of Blacks in America. To learn more about the life and thought of Elijah Muhammad, see Berg, 2009; Clegg, 1997; Essien-Udom, 1962; Halasa, 1993; Hakim, 1997; Pitre, 2021.

REFERENCES

Berg, H. (2009). *Elijah Muhammad and Islam*. New York University Press.

Clegg, C. (1997). *An original man: The life and thought of Elijah Muhammad*. St. Martin Press.

Essein-Udom, E.U. (1962). *Black Nationalism: A search for an identity in America*. The University of Chicago Press.

Farrakhan, L (2016 June 14). *A true friend: The honorable Elijah Muhammad*. http://www.finalcall.com/artman/publish/Minister_Louis_Farrakhan_9/A_True_Friend_1082.shtml

Hakim, N. (Ed.). (1997). *The true history of Elijah Muhammad: Messenger of Allah*. M.E.M.P.S.

Halasa, C. (1993). *Elijah Muhammad*. Chelsea Books.

Muhammad, E. (1965). *Message to the Blackman in America*. Final Call.

Muhammad, E. (1974). *Our savior has arrived*. Final Call.

Muhammad, E. (2006). *The theology of time*. M.E.M.P.S.

Muhammad, J. (1996). *This is the one: The most honored Elijah Muhammad*. Book Co.

Muhammad, T. (1996). *Chronology of Nation of Islam history: Highlights of the honorable minister Louis Farrakhan and the Nation of Islam from 1977–1996*. Steal Away Publications.

Pitre, A. (2021). *An introduction to Elijah Muhammad studies: The new educational paradigm* (rev ed.). Hamilton Books.

Sahib, H. A. (1951). The Nation of Islam [Unpublished master's thesis]. University of Chicago.

A Pedagogy of Liberation

Elijah Muhammad's entire mission was the reeducation of Blacks in America. And this reeducation was a pedagogy of liberation. He didn't use the traditional approach to education that focused on test scores. He poured out knowledge that touched the souls of his listeners.

Through narrative pedagogy, unlike the narration sickness described by Paulo Freire (2000), the knowledge he disclosed captivated his listeners. His students sat eagerly waiting to learn more about the sun or life on other planets. Mesmerized by these teachings, they sought out knowledge.

The narrative pedagogy afforded his students opportunities to reflect on their learning. For example, he would ask them to describe their perception of God. Then he would begin teaching on the reality of God. For perhaps the first time, students began to discover their voice. Unlike in public schools, where trickologists develop tricky questions designed to make students seem like failures, Muhammad appreciated hearing his students' perspectives.

The temples that he set up were, in reality, closer to mini universities that advanced students' educational status. Similar to a university, the learning at the mosque or temple closely resembled the type of education that took place in prestigious White institutions. The mosque served as a springboard to creating a desire and appetite for learning.

On Fridays, students would gather in a circle to discuss Muhammad's teachings. The circle, according to Elijah Muhammad, demonstrated that from zero, we get one. The shape of a 0 resembles an egg, something that has life but needs to evolve in order that it might come into another form of existence.

During these study sessions, students were asked to reflect on what they had been taught. This was the first time that many of the individuals who visited the mosque had the opportunity to reflect on their learning. Schooling for the most part had taken away their ability to think freely. Thinking was contrary to the slave-makers, who benefited from Black labor, which prompted educational theorists to question the selection of knowledge used in schools. By controlling what is studied, those ruling society have always influenced the thinking and actions of students.

In these study sessions, discussions began with the most important question that one could encounter as a student: Who is God? In order to answer this question, the student was asked to reflect on their perception of God. Elijah Muhammad taught that God is a man, thus making his students reexamine biblical text.

Elijah Muhammad's students were inspired to seek knowledge. His pedagogical practices stressed the importance of reflective study, and this is reflected by his statement, "We should take time and study what has and is being taught to us. Study the word and examine it, and if it be the truth lay to hold to it" (1965, p. 2). In searching for God, Muhammad guided the student to reexamine themselves in relationship to God:

> God is a man and we just cannot make him other than man, lest we make him an inferior one; for man's intelligence has no equal in other than man. His wisdom is infinite: capable of accomplishing what his brain can conceive. A spirit is subjected to us and not we to the spirit. (1965, p. 6)

By encouraging his students to hold intelligence in high esteem, he was stimulating the desire in his students to seek knowledge. The knowledge of God and one's self awakened the teacher within. Farrakhan (2004) summarized the power of Muhammad's educational program:

> The Most Honorable Elijah Muhammad caused his students to be critical thinkers. Malcolm X only went to the 8th grade of school; he never went to high school or college. I went with him to Harvard, Yale, and to the finest institutions where he debated the best minds that this country could produce—and he whipped them all, hands down, because he was a critical thinker. (p. 22)

In schools today, students are not posed this basic question of who God is, which lays the base for studying and mastering all of the disciplines. To know that God is force and power and everything in his creation bears witness to his wisdom is to engage in the first act of gaining true knowledge, which is power.

In declaring that God is a human being, Elijah Muhammad urged his students to become actors in the world rather than spectators. He taught that there is no limit to what you can accomplish when your mind is rooted in the wisdom of God.

Under Elijah Muhammad's philosophy, students discovered that true education begins with the self. This knowledge of one's self propels the student into motion, which is the basis for time.

The knowledge of God and one's self begins with the discipline of history. Who are you? How did you get here? What is the role of society in shaping you? What is the relationship between the self and others?

In guiding the student to reflect on their lived experiences, Elijah Muhammad was ultimately saying, *This is what you have been made by others, but who are you?* Freire (2000) pointed out that the oppressed have been made beings for others, which coincides with Muhammad's argument that Black people were deprived of a true knowledge of themselves.

In his research, Ogbu (1995) found that Black students who exhibited high intelligence were regarded as "acting White" by their peers. The belief that Black intelligence is "acting White" demonstrates the lack of knowledge of self among Black students.

Elijah Muhammad taught that in order to understand themselves, Black people must come to know that their history dates back trillions of years to when God created himself. This history can be studied by looking at God's creation and uncovering artifacts that prove the history of Black people. The following words of Elijah Muhammad (1965) illustrated the need for historical knowledge:

> Historian J.A. Rogers points out in his book that beyond the cotton fields of the South and long before the white man himself was a part of our planet, we were the original people ruling the earth, and according to the Holy Quran, we had governments superior to any we are experiencing today. Trace over the earth. Check back 5,000, 10,000, or 20,000 years ago. Look at history. Who were those people? They were our people. Today, we are confronted with proof of who is the original people and who shall live on this earth and call it their own. (pp. 34–35)

The first step in Elijah Muhammad's curriculum is becoming a historical thinker. This historical thinking lays a foundation for understanding other subjects. However, it is important to understand that the disciplines, according to Elijah Muhammad, are linked together and are inseparable. For example, in studying history we are also studying mathematics, which is also the study of science.

Elijah Muhammad discussed the science of how history is written. The Black man, according to Elijah Muhammad, writes history not after it happens, but 25,000 years in advance to coincide with the circumference of our earth.

He stated, "We have also 23 Gods that write and justify history once every 25,000 years. ... There are really 24 gods. This number is used whenever they make up history. The 23 Gods work and one does the analyzation and calculation of what they write" (Rassoull, 1992, pp. 113–114). This science of history provides a new way of looking at history; instead of studying history for the memorization of facts, history forms the foundation for us to become actors in the world in which we live.

Elijah Muhammad believed a major role of educators should be to address the study of Black history: "Educators should teach our people of the great history that was theirs before they were brought to America in shackles by slave-masters" (1965, p. 171). In addition to examining history, he taught about the origin of life. Throughout his teachings, he stressed the study of mathematics and science.

The foundation for Elijah Muhammad's concept of science began with how God created himself in the darkness of space and then produced a universe filled with life. What type of science was used to create life? Elijah Muhammad gave us some insight into this:

> The atom out of which man was created came from space. It was out in space where he originated. An atom of life was in the darkness and he came out of that atom that was in space. Now you may wonder: how did that atom get in space? The history of space teaches us that at one time it was nothing but darkness. If there had been light for us to use our glasses on, to find if there was an atom of life in the darkness, before the atom exploded to show what it was, we would tell you so. But we can't go that far. (Rassoull, 1992, p. 105)

Another example of the scientific knowledge of Elijah Muhammad deals with the sun and its powerful impact on the human family. Not only did Elijah Muhammad note that 6 trillion years passed before

God put the sun into use, but he also demonstrated the connection between human beings and the sun:

> It was 6 trillion years, so God taught me, before he put the sun into use. After the sun, other gods were born and they caught up the same idea: making something out of fire. Never have you known what and how fire came into space. The stars and a big star we call sun are nothing but balls of fire. I want you to remember these things so that you don't make a mistake. The God created himself out of matter that he took out of darkness of space. How, then can we declare that the fiery stars, along with our sun were created out of space? Where did the fire come from? Everything is full of fire. I am full of fire. You are full of fire. (Rassoull, 1992, pp. 108–109)

Elijah Muhammad's teachings stretched across disciplines and were transdisciplinary; each of the disciplines has been used to empower and address the problems facing Black people.

The Educational Mission

Elijah Muhammad's mission was to awaken Blacks in America to the seed of greatness that they embodied. In an interview, Muhammad (1965) specifically described his work: "My mission is to give life to the dead. What I teach brings them out of death and into life. ... This truth I bring will give you knowledge of yourself and your God" (p. 305). Muhammad's work was an educational undertaking whereby a people who had been destroyed mentally could be restored to their divinity.

What Muhammad was able to do with his students and others who have studied from afar is to bring to consciousness their potential to transform the world. Naim Akbar (1998) referenced this point when he said, "The major premise of effective education must be self-knowledge. In order to achieve the goals of identity and empowerment ... the educational process must be one that educes the awareness of who we are" (p. 17).

Elijah Muhammad's pedagogical practices brought out the potential in his students. His mission statement forms the foundation for true education. To lead one from ignorance into knowledge is to lead one from death into life. In finding life, one is able to find the essence of love.

Elijah Muhammad was deeply in love with Black people. He knew that many of the problems facing Blacks in America were a result of limited knowledge. When he wrote that the most important knowledge was of God and self, he was laying the foundation for human transformation (Muhammad, 1965).

A close examination of the current public-school agenda will reveal that in schools labeled "inner city," the presence of death is everywhere. The school curriculum is out of touch with the knowledge needed to help students understand the role of history in shaping the present situations they might face (Milner, 2019). In particular, the curriculum becomes sanitized so that the impact of racism is not examined (Milner, 2019; Nieto & Bode, 2018). The attack on critical race theory by politicians is one example of how those in positions of power influence curriculum. It is highly likely that some teachers in the 21st century have never studied the civil rights and Black Power movements in America.

The miseducation of educators has contributed to negative educational experiences for too many Black students. And the oppressive school culture experienced by Black students "is nourished by love of death, not life" (Freire, 2000, p. 76). Elijah Muhammad, realizing the potency of White supremacy, pleaded with Blacks not to integrate into this type of system lest they find themselves tricked.

During his 44 years of teaching in America, Elijah Muhammad had to patiently endure the pain that came with raising the consciousness of a people who had been put in a mental state of death. Like all of the great teachers and prophets who came before him, he had to suffer rejection from his own people. His life is a testament to the suffering experienced by teachers and messengers who disclosed knowledge that would free those suffering under oppression. His life was characterized by careful study, patience, suffering, and hope. Ultimately, his work can be summed up in one word: *love*.

Today we are confronted with all of the pressing issues that Elijah Muhammad raised over 80 years ago. This unlettered man from Georgia should be reexamined at this critical point in world history during which racial justice and Black lives are a national concern.

REFERENCES

Akbar, N. (1998). *Know thyself*. Mind Productions & Associates.

Farrakhan, L. (2004). *Passing the torch: The revival of youth activism and leadership*. http://www.finalcall.com/artman/publish/Minister_Louis_Farrakhan_9/Passing_the_torch_The_Revival_of_Youth_Activism_an_1633.shtml

Freire, P. (2000). *Pedagogy of the oppressed*. Continuum.

Milner, R. (2019). Race to improve teacher education: Building awareness for instructional practice. *American Educator, 3*, 13–17.

Muhammad, E. (1965). *Message to the Blackman in America*. Final Call.

Nieto, S., & Bode, P. (2018). *Affirming diversity: The sociopolitical context of multicultural education*. Pearson.

Ogbu, J. U. (1995). Understanding cultural diversity and learning. In J. A. Banks & C. A. McGee Banks (Eds.), *Handbook of research on multicultural education* (pp. 582–696). Macmillan.

Rassoull, A. (1992). *The theology of time: The most honorable Elijah Muhammad*. UBUS Communication.

SELECTION 1

Re-Educate the Blackman

Background

"Re-Educate the Blackman" discussed both the need for Blacks to be reeducated as well as the importance of education. In this selection, the seeds of Africana Studies are planted when Muhammad talks about Blacks learning about their history. He also wrote about land ownership, suggesting the importance of self-determination, which is one of the tenets of Africana Studies. Moreover, the selection highlights Elijah Muhammad's critique of Black education, disclosing that it did not prepare Blacks to be independent of their former slave masters.

Overview

In "Re-Educate the Blackman", Elijah Muhammad discussed the need for Blacks to be reeducated. After Blacks experienced chattel slavery for nearly 300 years, which included being denied the right to read, Muhammad wrote that the education Blacks were receiving was insufficient:

> The "up-from-slavery" education that the white man has given his once slave is not sufficient to set him free

from his slavemaster; because it is in the favor of the slave master to keep him in the power of the white man's civilization. Think it over.

Elijah Muhammad's assessment of Black education aligns with critical Black pedagogy. Critical Black pedagogy offers an African-centered critique of education with the intent of empowering Black people through education (Pitre, 2019). When schools were set up for Blacks in America after the Civil War, they were designed by the people who had enslaved them.

Elijah Muhammad's argument for the necessity of reeducation was on point considering these historical facts. Moreover, Elijah Muhammad argued that the enslavement of Blacks in America entailed robbing them of their knowledge of self. For Elijah Muhammad, robbing Black people of knowledge was the worst crime that could be committed against them.

Reeducation of Blacks in America would include providing knowledge of their historical past dating back to ancient civilizations (e.g., learning about ancient Egypt and the Nile Valley civilizations). Elijah Muhammad believed that if Blacks learned about their historical greatness, it would allow them to unite with Black people all over the earth. Malcolm X articulated these teachings when he said, "Just as a tree without roots is dead, a people without history or cultural roots also becomes a dead people" (Pitre, 2019, p. 63).

The reeducation program that Elijah Muhammad envisioned is best seen in the discipline of Africana Studies, which is now offered in colleges and universities. In every course that is offered in Africana Studies, the teachings of Elijah Muhammad can be applied. Africana Studies was born as a result of the Black Power movement of the 1960s, which was heavily influenced by the Nation of Islam, and in particular, the work of Malcolm X (Karenga, 2002). Malcolm X was a student of Elijah Muhammad and in fact articulated what he learned from him.

Today, Africana Studies is defined as "an academic discipline that seeks to investigate phenomena and interrogate issues of the world from an African-centered perspective. The results should be transposed into communally relevant data which will ultimately empower the African community physically, psychologically and spiritually" (Norment, 2019, p. 12). Maulana Karenga, one of the founders of Black Studies, who was influenced by Malcolm X, has defined Black/Africana Studies as "the systematic and critical study of the multidimensional aspects of Black thought and practice in their current and historical unfolding. It is a critical study in that it is characterized by careful analysis and considered judgement. And it is systematic in that it is structured and methodical in its pursuit of knowledge and presentation of knowledge". (Karenga, 2002, p. 3)

Africana Studies offers what Elijah Muhammad envisioned: an opportunity for Black people to study the self.

Reeducation was also important according to Elijah Muhammad because there was going to be a final war that would end White rule throughout the earth. In order for Blacks to assume leadership in the new world that would emerge after this war, they would have to clean themselves from the vices that left them spiritually blind.

The current entertainment industry that uses silent weapons to make suggestions to the human mind that lead to self-destruction would have to be discarded. He wrote, "It is a shame to observe the type of knowledge that the Black Man of America displays. And, the greatest percentage is indecency." Muhammad taught that Blacks in America did not know that they were living in the time of judgment: "He must know the time and change that is now in the workings. He must know who has the Power of this change of worlds. He cannot build a future with white people in his mind."

For Elijah Muhammad, reeducation was both physical and spiritual: "*They must wash themselves up internally and externally,* as well, to join in or become members of the best societies of the Nations of the earth" (emphasis added). The current practices that include vulgar language and the use of drugs and alcohol that rob the thinking process and ultimately lead to death would not be transferred to the new world. He wrote, "If you think, Brother, that you can carry the evil and filth of this world over into the Hereafter, you are greatly mistaken."

Lastly, the reeducation of Blacks in America would need to stress the value of land ownership. By owning land, Black people would be able to provide for themselves the things they needed to survive without depending on their former slave masters. Muhammad closed his writing on reeducation by asking for help:

> HELP ME with whatever finance you can spare to build an Educational Center to re-educate you. I have, at my side, the best teachers and scientists of the Nations of the earth to staff a new educational center. Rise up and help me to do good things for you and God will bless you with success all the days of your life.

Elijah Muhammad believed that the reeducation of Blacks in America was important considering the devastating psychological effects of their enslavement in America. His ideas for the reeducation of Blacks in America led to what is now called Africana Studies. Moreover, Africana Studies became the foundation of ethnic studies. The teachings of Elijah Muhammad are applicable to every course offered in Africana Studies programs.

DISCUSSION QUESTIONS

After reading the overview of "Re-Educate the Blackman," think about what is being said about the politics of education and what it means for Africana Studies.

1. What are some key things that you have learned in this selection that speak to who decides what is taught in schools and universities?
2. Can you highlight how this selection was a forerunner to Africana Studies?
3. What are three major things that you have learned from this selection?

TEST YOUR KNOWLEDGE

True or False?

1. Elijah Muhammad believed Blacks in America were not deprived of the knowledge of self.
2. The study of Ancient Egypt and the Nile Valley civilization were part of Elijah Muhammad's teachings.
3. The current popular culture that promotes vulgar language and unhealthy lifestyles was addressed in Elijah Muhammad's teachings.
4. Elijah Muhammad's teachings are not applicable to some areas of study within the discipline of Africana studies.

REFERENCES

Karenga, M. (2002). *An introduction to Black studies*. The University of Sankore Press.

Muhammad, E. (1973, January 26). Re-Educate the Blackman. *Muhammad Speaks*, 12(20).

Norment, N. (2019). *African American studies: The discipline and its dimensions*. Peter Lang.

Pitre, A. (Ed.). (2019). *A critical Black pedagogy reader: The brothers speak*. Rowman and Littlefield.

SELECTION 2

Who Is That Mystery God?

Background

"Who Is That Mystery God?" is the foundation of the Nation of Islam's teaching, declaring that God is a human being with supreme knowledge and is a Black man. It entails a critique of dominant religious belief about the reality of God. Questions about God have also been the foundation from which great educational institutions began. Oxford University, the oldest university in Europe, has as its motto "The Lord is my light" (Psalm 27). Moreover, "Who Is That Mystery God?" is designed to make the reader reflect on their perception of God and how it affects the way they perceive and value education. The disclosure that God is a human being inspired Elijah Muhammad's followers to become seekers of knowledge.

Overview

In "Who Is That Mystery God?" Elijah Muhammad began with the most important question that one could ask: Who is God? Elijah Muhammad believed the knowledge of God should be the first step in the education of Blacks in America. His belief that God should be included in the education discourse aligns with many scholars of Africana Studies who write that God is at the center of education for Black people (Akbar, 1998).

In part, the education of Blacks in America included a theology that portrayed images of White men as being divine but at the same time taught that God was a mystery, a spook that no one could see. Elijah Muhammad offered a counter to the narrative of whiteness being divine. He began by saying that for thousands of years people did not possess the knowledge or reality of God, and as result, they began to develop their own ideas about God.

In the Christian world, Blacks were taught that God is a mystery and a spirit. Muhammad challenged the European construction of Christianity by saying:

> The Christians refer to God as a "Mystery" and a "Spirit" and divide Him into thirds. One part they call the Father, another part the Son, and the third part they call the Holy Ghost; which makes the three, one. This is contrary to both nature and mathematics.
>
> The law of mathematics will not allow us to put three into one. Our nature rebels against such a belief of God being a mystery and yet the Father of a son and a Holy Ghost without a wife or without being something in reality. We wonder how can the son be human, and the father a mystery (unknown), or a spirit? Who is this Holy Ghost that is classified as being the equal of the father and the son?

He then goes on to say that Christians don't believe God is a human being, but yet they refer to God with words such as *He*, *Him*, *Man*, *King*, and *The Ruler*. In addition, the Bible says that God grieves, he walks and talks, and that man is made in the likeness of God, but not human. For

Elijah Muhammad, the Eurocentric construction of Christianity contradicted writings found in the Bible.

For example, it could be argued that Elijah Muhammad's teaching that God is a human being is not contrary to Christian belief. Perhaps the majority of people have not thought deeply about who God is or the possibility of God being a human being. The Bible aligns with Elijah Muhammad's teaching that God is a human being. For example, Philippians 2:7 states, "But [God] made himself of no reputation, and took upon him the form of a servant, and was made in the likeness of men."

Elijah Muhammad challenged Christian theologians by raising the question of how one can teach about God if they declare that He is a mystery. He then defined the term *mystery*, noting that it means "something that is unknown." Afterward he asks, if *mystery* means "unknown," how would it be possible to teach what one doesn't know? He cogently asked the following questions:

> Can God be a Mystery God and yet send prophets to represent Himself? Have the prophets been representing a God that is not known (Mystery)? They tell us that they heard God's voice speaking to them in their own language. Can a spirit speak a language while being an immaterial something? If God is not material, what pleasure would He get out of material beings and the material universe? What is the basis of spirit? Is the spirit independent of material?
>
> Actually, who is that Mystery God? We should take time and study what has and is being taught to us. Study the word and examine it, and if it be the Truth, lay hold to it. To teach people that God is a Mystery God is to teach them that God is unknown. There is no truth in such teaching. Can one teach that which he himself does not know?

Muhammad went on to argue that the teaching of God being a mystery originated with Yakub, the Black god of the White man's creation. Yakub was a Black scientist who at the age of six developed the idea to produce a man that was the opposite of the Black man. Through a grafting process that included laborers, it took 600 years to produce the White race.

Yakub was a doctor who studied genetics and a was a master of organizational principles. After producing the White man, he was taught how to rule aboriginal people. When Elijah Muhammad referred to Whites as the devil, he meant grafted men. He wrote that any time you graft from the original, it is called devil.

The White man, by teaching that God is a mystery, would rule Blacks for 6,000 years, until they [Blacks] produced a God with a greater knowledge than Yakub and the men he produced. Regarding the origin of the teachings that God is a mystery, Muhammad wrote:

> the origin of such teachings as a Mystery God is from the devils! It was taught to them by their father, Yakub, 6,000 years ago. They know today that God is not a mystery but will not teach it. He (devil), the god of evil, was made to rule the nations of earth for 6,000 years, and naturally he would not teach obedience to a God other than himself.

Elijah Muhammad's teaching that the originator of the heavens and earth is a Black God, a human being, disrupted White supremacy and caused Blacks and Whites to look anew at themselves. It also stimulated in Black people a thirst for knowledge of themselves. After gaining this and other bodies of knowledge found in the Holy Qur'an, Blacks could then begin to hear the inner voice, the voice of God that had been asleep in them. This would allow their creative genius to emerge and give birth to a world that no one had ever seen before. However, under Western education, Blacks would continue to be a tool for those ruling society.

Black labor would be used to the benefit of business owners, who would pay a minimum wage for their labor while becoming rich.

The revelation that God is a human being and, moreover, a Black man who appeared to liberate Blacks from their oppressors was the cornerstone of Elijah Muhammad's teachings. A perusal of Africana Studies literature demonstrates that Elijah Muhammad was correct when he disclosed that the Black man is the originator of civilization (Karenga, 2002). When Elijah Muhammad was challenged by those who believed God was a mystery, he would simply say something along these lines: "Who produced that car you are driving? Who produced that cell phone that you are using? Is it not a man?" He would then go on to say, "I can show you what man has produced, but can you show me what your mystery has produced?" When closing a prayer, his students have noted the following words are said: "A-men" or "A-man."

DISCUSSION QUESTIONS

As you reflect on Elijah Muhammad's teachings from "Who Is That Mystery God?" that God is not only a human being but more so a Black man, respond to the following questions:

1. Have you ever given any thought to who God is and what your perception of God is?
2. How do you think Elijah Muhammad envisioned the knowledge of God empowering Black people?
3. How does the information in this selection dismantle White supremacy?
4. What are three things that stood out to you in this selection?

TEST YOUR KNOWLEDGE

True or False?

1. The knowledge of God was not addressed by Elijah Muhammad.

2. Elijah Muhammad taught that Yakub, a Black scientist, brought Whites into existence through a grafting process.
3. According to Elijah Muhammad, White rule would last beyond 6,000 years.
4. A perusal of literature from Africana studies would support Elijah Muhammad's teaching that Blacks are the original people.

REFERENCES

Akbar, N. (1998). *Know thyself.* Mind Productions and Associates.

Karenga, M. (2002). *An introduction to Black studies.* The University of Sankore Press.

Muhammad, E. (2003). *The genius of Elijah Muhammad: Unpublished and rare writings of Elijah Muhammad (Messenger of Allah) 1959–1962.* Secretarius Publications.

SELECTION 3

Know Thyself

Background

"Know Thyself" admonished Blacks to gain knowledge of themselves. The knowledge of self has many dimensions and evolves over time. Knowing one's self leads to higher levels of consciousness, and the concept has similarities to culturally relevant pedagogy (Ladson-Billings, 2021). The entire teachings of Elijah Muhammad were based on a body of knowledge specific to the needs of Black people. This selection critiqued the way of life that Blacks were living under, arguing that it is foreign to them. It pointed out the role of racism and White supremacy in creating a culture that kept Black people from discovering their creative genius. "Know Thyself" demonstrated how the teachings of Elijah Muhammad were also a precursor to African-centered education, which explores all fields and disciplines of study from the perspective of Black people (Asante, 1991). The knowledge of self made all the disciplines of study relevant.

Overview

"Know Thyself" was one of the most significant writings of Elijah Muhammad (Van Deburg, 1997) and is full of insight for those seeking to educate Black people. In K–12 schools, there are questions around how to improve the educational experiences of Black students. While many of these questions are the result of what is described as an achievement gap, which is based on test scores, Elijah Muhammad offered a teaching strategy that could be the basis of education for Blacks in America beyond current K–12 schools and universities. Elijah Muhammad's teachings were not elitist but were applicable to Black people wherever they may be found because they are intended to empower Blacks to discover their greatness.

Michael Apple (2019), a leading curriculum scholar, has talked about the selective tradition. In describing the selective tradition, he pointed out how those in power select the knowledge that is used in schools. He also disclosed that curriculum scholars ask what knowledge is most important for students to know. Elijah Muhammad shattered the contemporary foundations on which education is built. Today's education is based on human capitalist economics: the belief that schools should be concerned with preparing future workers (Spring, 2016). Human capitalist ideology is fueled by the super-rich, who create think tanks and foundations to shape educational policy.

Elijah Muhammad offered a key for the liberation of Black people when he declared, "Know Thyself." He boldly asserted why the knowledge of self was important:

> It is knowledge of self that the so-called Negroes lack which keeps them from enjoying freedom, justice and equality. This belongs to them divinely as much as it does to other nations of the earth.
>
> It is Allah's (God's) will and purpose that we shall know ourselves. Therefore, He came Himself to teach us the knowledge of self. Who is better knowing of who we are than God, Himself?

In the language of *Black liberation theology*, he disclosed that God had come to bring knowledge that would empower Blacks in America (Cone, 2010 [1970]). This knowledge could be traced back to the tribe of Shabazz. Regarding the tribe of Shabazz, he wrote that they came with the earth (or this part) 66 trillion years ago when a great explosion on our planet divided it into two parts. One we call earth and the other moon.

> This was done by one of our scientists, God, who wanted the people to speak one language, one dialect for all, but was unable to bring this about. He decided to kill us by the destroying our planet, but still He failed. We were lucky to be on this part, earth, which did not lose its water in the mighty blasting away of the part called moon.

> We, the tribe of Shabazz, says Allah (God), were the first to discover the best part of our planet to live on. The rich Nile Valley of Egypt and the present seat of the Holy City, Mecca, Arabia.

In his description of the tribe of Shabazz, he mentioned the rich Nile Valley civilizations of Egypt. Study of the Nile Valley of Egypt is a cornerstone of Africana Studies. It could be argued that Africana Studies courses on ancient Egypt were influenced by Elijah Muhammad's teachings.

Elijah Muhammad traced the origin of the Black man beyond 66 trillion years to the making of the moon. He described the heavenly bodies as not just something that appeared but were produced by Black people who possessed a particular kind of knowledge.

By teaching Black people the knowledge of self, he wanted to dislodge the oppressor consciousness they possessed. For example, it was common for some Blacks to believe White was good and Black was evil. For the most part, many Blacks had come to believe their phenotype was the worst kind to be possessed among humans. Elijah Muhammad countered the prevailing belief that Black was ugly, writing:

> The origin of our kinky hair, says Allah, came from one of our dissatisfied scientists, 50,000 years ago, who wanted to make all of us tough and hard in order to endure the life of the jungles of East Asia (Africa) and to overcome the beasts there. But he failed to get the others to agree with him.
>
> He took his family and moved into the jungle to prove to us that we could live there and conquer the wild beasts, and we have. So, being the first and the smartest scientist on the deportation of our moon and the one who suffered most of all, Allah (God) has decided to place us on the top with a thorough knowledge of self and his guidance.

According to Elijah Muhammad, the knowledge of self is the basis for true liberation. He believed that a careful study of Black history would help Blacks discover their potential for greatness. He taught that the origin of all people is from the Black man and woman: "To know thyself is to know all men, as from us came all and to us all will return."

He also urged Blacks in America to give up the names of their former slave masters. In keeping their slave masters' names, Black people kept themselves in psychological chains. The teachings of Elijah Muhammad gave birth to Black psychology by influencing the work of one of the premiere Black psychologists, Naim Akbar (1996), who wrote a book titled *Breaking the Chains of Psychological Slavery*.

DISCUSSION QUESTIONS

The knowledge of self was a cornerstone in the teachings of Elijah Muhammad. In "Know Thyself," a discussion of the Nile Valley and Egypt are highlighted. Today, the Africana Studies curriculum includes the ancient history of Blacks prior to their arrival to the Americas.

1. What does having "knowledge of self" mean to you?
2. How does depriving the masses of knowledge about the historical greatness of Black people contribute to racism and inequality?
3. Why do you think Elijah Muhammad critiqued the names Black people held?
4. What are three main things that stood out to you from this selection?

TEST YOUR KNOWLEDGE

True or False?

1. Elijah Muhammad's teachings did not address ancient Egypt and the Nile Valley civilization.
2. Elijah Muhammad believed the knowledge of self was key to Black education.
3. According to Elijah Muhammad's teachings, the origin of Black people dates back thousands of years.
4. Elijah Muhammad's teachings influenced Black psychology.

REFERENCES

Akbar, N. (1996). *Breaking the chains of psychological slavery*. Mind Productions and Associates.

Apple, M. (2019). *Ideology and curriculum* (4th ed.). Routledge.

Asante, M. K. (1991). The Afrocentric idea in education. *Journal of Negro Education, 60*(2), 170–179.

Cone, J. (2010). *A Black theology of liberation.* Oribis Books. (Original work published 1970)

Muhammad, E. (1965). Original man, know thyself. In *Message to the Blackman in America.* Muhammad's Temple of Islam No. 2.

Ladson-Billings, G. (2021). Fighting for our lives: Preparing teachers to teach African American students. In A. Pitre, T. Hudson, J. Smith-Gray, & K. James (Eds.), *The Gloria Ladson-Billings reader* (pp. 172–184). Cognella.

Spring, J. H. (2016). *Deculturalization and the struggle for equality: Brief history of the education of dominated cultures in the United States.* Routledge.

Van Deburg, William L. (1997). *Modern Black nationalism: From Marcus Garvey to Louis Farrakhan.* NYU Press.

SELECTION 4

Get Knowledge to Benefit Self

Background

In "Get Knowledge to Benefit Self," Muhammad stressed that gaining knowledge of one's self stimulates the desire to learn. He highlighted how knowledge of self can create unity among Black people, and he encouraged Blacks to get an education that would cause them to become job producers rather than laborers for the White owners of industry. The selection highlights the selective tradition, which asked questions like, *Who decides what knowledge is used in schools?* and *Whose knowledge is selected for study in the curriculum?* (Apple, 2019). Using historical facts, he shared a debate in Congress regarding what bodies of knowledge would be taught to Blacks in America. The selection concludes with a very powerful definition of *knowledge*.

Overview

In "Get Knowledge to Benefit Self," Elijah Muhammad demonstrated why he is one of the premiere critical Black pedagogues. His disclosure of what knowledge is of most importance lays the foundation for Black education. Opposed to accepting the slogan "Get a good education," Elijah Muhammad taught what a good education entails.

He says that in getting knowledge, or what we now call "an education," Blacks in America first needed the knowledge of self. He then explained that Blacks in America were like amnesia victims because they did not know themselves. This argument gave birth to the necessity of Black/Africana Studies. Secondly, Elijah Muhammad believed that the knowledge of self would inspire Black people and that it would create unity among them:

> Anyone who does not have a knowledge of self is considered a victim of either amnesia or unconsciousness and is not very competent. The lack of knowledge of self is a prevailing condition among my people here in America. Gaining the knowledge of self makes us unite into a great unity. Knowledge of self makes you take on the great virtue of learning.

At the time of his writing, there were those who attempted to degrade Muslims because they were teaching what appeared to be something strange. This led to the famed documentary by Mike Wallace and Louis Lomax (1959) titled, *The Hate That Hate Produced*, which aired on national television. It was the first time that the masses of people in America were exposed to the teachings of the so-called "Black Muslims." Because many of the followers of Elijah Muhammad did not attend mainstream universities, they were considered unlettered or unschooled.

This caused Elijah Muhammad to declare that no other followers were more zealous about learning than his, as "throughout the Holy Qur'an, the duty of a Muslim to acquire knowledge is spelled out."

He went on to discuss the importance of Black people getting an education that would benefit them as a group. Education for Black people would not entail them giving their talent and labor to the White owners who were exploiting them. Moreover, education would empower Blacks by stimulating them with the idea to produce jobs for themselves. They would not be looking to work for Fortune 500 companies because their education would empower them to create their own companies:

> We need education, but an education which removes us from the shackles of slavery and servitude. Get an education, but not an education which leaves us in an inferior position and without a future. Get an education, but not an education that leaves us looking to the slave-master for a job.

The idea of becoming a business owner made Elijah Muhammad one of the most disliked Black leaders of his time. He was offering Black people a path toward true liberation because he understood that it was business owners who ruled the country. Joel Spring, in his book *The Politics of American Education* (2011), discussed the power of business owners to influence education policy.

Regarding the issue of integration, Elijah Muhammad did not believe Black children should be integrated into predominantly White schools. In part, the Eurocentric perspective that White educators would carry to the classroom would prove detrimental to Black students.

Today, overrepresentation of Black students in special education, higher suspension rates, and lower self-esteem can be partially attributed to the dominant White female teaching force that may have negative perceptions of Black people. As a result of these perceptions, such as low expectations and fear of Black youth taking leadership roles, such teachers create negative learning experiences for Black students, particularly Black boys, who are treated like adults when punishment is meted out (Ladson-Billings, 2011).

The negative learning experiences of Black boys are similar to what George Floyd experienced on the streets of Minnesota, where he cried out, "Get your knee off my neck!" Schools today mirror Woodson's (2010 [1933]) argument that the worst sort of lynching occurred in the schools, where instead of the greatness of Black people being taught, Black students were being taught their Blackness was a curse.

Elijah Muhammad recognized this problem and pointed out that Black children need to spend the first 15–16 years of their education in Black schools. In this way he felt they would not lose their identity. "No people strive to lose themselves among other people except the so-called American Negroes," he wrote. "This they do because of their lack of knowledge of self."

In describing the importance of Blacks in America using their education to benefit themselves as a collective, Muhammad discussed foreign exchange students who come to America for education. After receiving education, they take what they have learned back to their countries for the benefit of their people. Likewise, Blacks in America should take what they have learned and use it to the benefit of their people in America. He questioned those who were critiquing him by asking, "Why is scorn and abuse directed toward my followers and myself when we say our people should get an education which will aid, benefit and uplift our people?"

Elijah Muhammad was a threat to White rule because his ideas about the purpose of Black education contrasted with those of the White ruling class. In a powerful statement on Black education, he declared, "Get an education, but one which will instill the ideas and desire to get something of your own, a country of your own and jobs of your own."

Blacks in America didn't foresee education as the pathway to getting a country of their own. The idea of getting a country of their own would lead to producing money that would have pictures of Black people on it. Their creative expression would produce a world that had never been seen before. The diseases afflicting the world could be solved by Black genius. The Black god power that was asleep in Black people would be awakened because their education would be premised on producing ideas. It would not entail trickology.

Trickology involves testing that is heavily invested in trying to trick the student into a wrong answer. For Elijah Muhammad, testing would be used to bring out Black genius. Just like Black sports figures and entertainers who are on display for the world, the Black genius would produce cars and buildings never seen before.

Elijah Muhammad also disclosed the origin of the problem of Black education. Black education has been under the control of what William Watkins (2001) called the White architects of Black education. Watkins pointed out that after the Civil War, these White architects designed a 75-year plan for educating Blacks.

Prior to modern scholars of educational history, Elijah Muhammad wrote about a debate that was taking place regarding funding for Howard University, a historically black college in Washington, DC. In that meeting, a congressman declared there would not be a need to appropriate money for Howard University because they would not educate Black people in the science of warfare (military science), birth control, or chemistry. Elijah Muhammad wrote that those in power knew that these bodies of knowledge were necessary for Blacks to be free. Using the language of critical pedagogy, he wrote:

> This shows the slave-master has been very successful in dominating us with an education beneficial to him. There is a saying among us, "Mother may have, father may have, but God blesses the child who has its own." It is time we had our own.

Today, the education of Black people is controlled by a White ruling class. Despite the fact there are several Blacks who hold leadership roles in education, it is like the saying goes: it doesn't matter who plays the game—the rules remain the same. Elijah Muhammad envisioned Black education that was outside the scope of the mainstream perspective. He brilliantly described what Black education should be: an education that lets Blacks exercise freedom, elevates them, and eliminates division among them.

As it relates to curriculum, he believed Black education should go beyond the "three R's" (reading, writing, and arithmetic) to include "the history of the black nation, the knowledge of civilization of man and the universe and all the sciences." This is, in essence, Africana Studies when it is not watered down.

In closing, Muhammad believed education should elevate Blacks and that those who were teachers should be compensated because they would play a major role in uplifting Black people. For Muhammad, it was knowledge that Black people needed most. He connected knowledge to God, offering a definition of *knowledge* that is matchless:

> One of the attributes of Allah, The All-Wise God, Who is the Supreme Being, is knowledge. Knowledge is the result of learning and is a force or energy that makes its bearer accomplish or overcome obstacles, barriers and resistance. In fact, God means possessor or power and force. The education my people need is that knowledge, the attribute of God, which creates power to accomplish and make progress in the good things or the righteous things.

DISCUSSION QUESTIONS

"Get Knowledge to Benefit Self" discussed education as a way to empower Blacks (critical pedagogy) and discussed the history of Black education in a capitalist society.

1. What are three things in this selection that stand out to you? Briefly explain why these were important to you.
2. Can you identify how this selection relates to Africana Studies?
3. Can you think of ways that the education of Black people is still directed by those in power?

4. What do you think is meant by "knowledge creates power to accomplish and make progress in the good things or the righteous things"?

TEST YOUR KNOWLEDGE

True or False?

1. Elijah Muhammad believed education should empower Blacks to produce jobs and a country for themselves.
2. The White ruling class of America supported Elijah Muhammad's educational philosophy.
3. The debate over what to include in the curriculum at Howard University demonstrates how those in power were committed to using education as tool to empower Blacks in America.
4. Elijah Muhammad believed gaining knowledge was an attribute of God.

REFERENCES

Apple, M. (2019). *Ideology and curriculum* (4th ed.). Routledge.

Ladson-Billings, G. (2011). Boyz to men? Teaching to restore Black boys' childhood. *Race, Ethnicity and Education, 14*(1), 7–15.

Muhammad, Elijah. (2012). *The foundation years of Elijah Muhammad 1958–1962* (Volumes 1 & 2). Secretarius Incorporated.

Spring, J. H. (2011). *The politics of American education*. Routledge.

Wallace, M., & Lomax, L. (1959, July 13–17). *The hate that hate produced* [five-part docuseries]. Distributed by WNTA-TV.

Watkins, W. (2001). *The White architects of Black education: Ideology and power in America, 1865–1954*. Teachers College Press.

Woodson, C. G. (2010). *The mis-education of the Negro*. UBUS Communication. (Original work published 1933.)

SELECTION 5

If the Civilized Man Fails to Perform His Duty, What Must Be Done?

Background

"If the Civilized Man Fails to Perform His Duty, What Must Be Done?" discussed the importance of having spiritual teachers who possess understanding of Black consciousness. Muhammad encouraged his students to use their newly acquired knowledge to uplift Blacks by teaching. Teaching was a crusade that would usher in the transformation of Black lives. For Elijah Muhammad, the act of teaching was a spiritual undertaking. In critiquing the education of Blacks, he asked if their education was equal to that of their slave-masters, meaning the White ruling class. He went on to say that those controlling the education of Black people would not educate them for freedom.

Overview

In "If the Civilized Man Fails to Perform His Duty, What Must Be Done?" Elijah Muhammad addressed the importance of having teachers who were equipped with the knowledge of self. He pointed out that in preparation programs, future educators are not exposed to

African-centered perspectives of education. In addition, educators very seldom learn about the great African civilizations that pre-date European ones.

Elijah Muhammad believed it was the duty of teachers to advance Black people. Black education is connected to concepts found in *Black Liberation Theology (Cone, 2010)*. In Black liberation theology, God appears to free those suffering under oppression. The freedom of oppressed people is connected to the knowledge they receive by way of a Divine Messenger.

The condition of Black people due to their being robbed of the knowledge of self would require them to have a teacher who was prepared and commissioned by God. This Divine Messenger would share a knowledge that would be like the *Sun* in that it would awaken and bring to life to those languishing under oppression.

The Divine Messenger would teach high spiritual science that would make a spiritual civilization. Unlike the beast or savage mind that is often glorified in the contemporary world, Elijah Muhammad believed "well-educated, cultured and courteous people make a beautiful society when it is spiritual. Good manners come from the civilized man who does not fail to perform his duty."

In his discussion of civilizations, he pointed out that the one we currently live under is filled with wickedness. If one were to turn on radio stations in Black communities, they would find some of the filthiest language one can imagine. Black youth today sometimes refer to themselves as *savage* and *beast*. Elijah Muhammad declared in the 1930s that his teachings were designed to bring Black people out of a savage condition. Who would have imagined that in 2021 Black popular culture in America would be premised on the denigration of Black people?

According to Muhammad, the savagery that is on display by Blacks in America is a testament to the education they have received under White rule, which failed to civilize Blacks. Moreover, Elijah Muhammad taught about the role of education in enslaving Black people. Equal education, he argued, was not provided to Blacks, as Whites still persecute Blacks who try to learn about themselves and their culture. Those seeking to liberate Black people through education encountered a counter to intelligence, which led to the FBI's Counterintelligence Program that sought to destroy Black leaders, chief among them Elijah Muhammad.

Muhammad pointed out that it was also fear of White people that stopped Black people from being free. He cites fear of hunger, homelessness, and friendship from Whites, as reasons preventing Blacks from seeking freedom. With regards to education as the means for liberation, he wrote, "Separation of the so-called Negroes from their slave-masters' children is a must." Muhammad argued that without equal education, Blacks were still not free. Allah would provide knowledge and a country separate from White influence.

In closing, Muhammad disclosed why Blacks should not depend on those in positions of power to educate them:

> Who are you waiting for to teach you the knowledge of self? Surely not your slave-masters who blinded you to the knowledge. The white race's civilization will never work for us.

DISCUSSION QUESTIONS

This selection addresses the role of teachers in liberating Blacks. It offers a critique of education that entails the need for spiritual teachers but also discusses the persecutions liberator teachers will face.

1. Can you provide examples of cases in which educators have been punished for teaching Africana Studies courses in K–12 schools or universities?
2. What are your thoughts about Black people being schooled but not really educated in K–12 schools and universities?
3. What are three things that stood out to you in this selection?

TEST YOUR KNOWLEDGE

True or False?

1. The preparation of teachers who embodied a Black consciousness was important to Elijah Muhammad.
2. Elijah Muhammad believed that highly educated people should have a courteous disposition.
3. According to Elijah Muhammad, the job of the teacher is to awaken the creative mind.
4. Elijah Muhammad thought that those seeking to empower Blacks through education would be supported by the government.

REFERENCES

Cone, J. (2010). *A Black theology of liberation*. Oribis Books. (Original work published 1970.)

Muhammad, Elijah. (1956, August 4). "If the civilized man fails to perform his duty what must be done?" *Pittsburgh Courier*.

SELECTION 6

Beautiful Appearance and Long Life

Background

In "Beautiful Appearance and Long Life," Muhammad discussed the role of food in a spiritual context. He explained that not only does physical food affect one's appearance, it also affects the way one thinks. It becomes important to guard the words that one feeds the mind because they can influence the way we act. A discussion of food has been one of the glaring omissions in the discourse on Black education. Muhammad's discussion on food is particularly relevant to Black communities, where liquor and cigarette stores often prevail along with a shortage of healthy foods. The numerous liquor and smoke stores in Black communities and the absence of bookstores are indicators of how hegemony works.

Overview

In the study of education, there is a dearth of discourse with regards to the impact of food on the learning process. Elijah Muhammad addressed not only the spiritual but also the physical realities confronting Black people. He wrote two books (volumes 1 and 2) titled

How to Eat to Live. In both books, he offered a guide to eating that had not been previously known among Black people.

The Black Muslims, as they are called, were said to look different because they follow a diet that is not like the masses of people. In the discourse around *How to Eat to Live*, the teachings of Elijah Muhammad can be found in Africana Studies courses that address health issues in the Black community. Elijah Muhammad taught that eating one meal a day would lengthen one's life. He wrote that eating three times a day and in between meals changes one's appearance. According to the teachings of Elijah Muhammad, food impacts not only the physical appearance but also the way people think. He wrote:

> Beauty appearance is destroyed in us—not just our facial appearance, but the most beautiful appearance about us, our characteristics (the way we act and practice our way of life). We achieve one of the greatest beauties when we achieve the spiritual beauty and characteristics through practicing them. We achieve the spiritual beauty through practicing or carrying into practice the spiritual laws.
>
> We know that we have been made ugly by our enemies' rearing of our parents. We know that many of our people throughout the earth have been made ugly by not practicing culture that would beautify them. But we are blessed that God, Himself, has visited us to guide us in His way. What people on the earth has God visited in person today, other than you and me here in America?

With regards to poisonous food and water, he warned Blacks that if what they eat keeps them alive, it can also bring death. In part, he explained that the problem with the dietary habits of Black people is that they have been trained to eat by those who enslaved them. Kevin

Muhammad (2003) called the diet that Black people followed "a slave diet." In his book, *Slave Diet: Disease and Reparations*, he wrote that many of the foods that Black people eat today are a result of their enslavement, because they did not consume those foods in Africa. The American diet was the complete opposite of the African diet, and for the most part, Blacks were given the worst foods to eat during their enslavement.

The poison in food and water was foretold by Elijah Muhammad. For example, in the past, the majority of people would drink water from the faucet, but today, bottled water is bought from stores. With regards to these issues, Elijah Muhammad wrote:

> Poisonous food and water we are now eating and drinking—sometimes too much poison to kill poison that is in our food and drinks. And, maybe it is the wrong poison for us human beings, whether it is in food or in drinks.
>
> Take, for instance, the use of fluoride, chloride, and sodium, which if not used correctly can destroy our entire life. Maybe it is best to find something else that will clear our water without killing both us and the poison in our food and water.

Elijah Muhammad believed that the desire for money over the health needs of the American people has been detrimental:

> We live in a world commercializing on everything where money is involved, and this has speeded production of everything but human lives, in order to fill the demand of the people. This has caused many scientists to overlook the dangerous effects that such fast production has on the health of the people. Therefore, the only way out

for us, the poor Lost-Found, is to seek refuge and guidance in Allah for our protection from evil plannings and doings of Satan.

Elijah Muhammad's teachings included addressing the health issues impacting Black people. These health concerns led him to teach about what foods to eat, the times one should eat, and the number of times to eat per day.

DISCUSSION QUESTIONS

In "Beautiful Appearance and Long Life," Elijah Muhammad discussed the importance of healthy lifestyle choices and pointed out ways that institutional inequities make these choices difficult for Black people.

1. Can you think of any contemporary examples of institutional inequity that have led to poor health outcomes for Black Americans?
2. Why do you think Muhammad felt that this topic was worthy of discussion? What are his hopes for his readers?
3. What are three things that have caused you to reflect on your health?

TEST YOUR KNOWLEDGE

True or False?

1. Elijah Muhammad believed that the type of food people consume has nothing to do with their education.
2. Elijah Muhammad taught that eating food impacts people's physical appearance and thought processes.
3. According to Elijah Muhammad, eating several meals a day and drinking liquor was not harmful.
4. Elijah Muhammad identified the desire for money as being detrimental to the health needs of the American people.

REFERENCES

Muhammad, E. (2008). *How to eat to live*. Secretarius MEMPS Publications. (Original work published 1967.)

Muhammad, K. (2003). *The slave diet: Disease and reparations*. Tech Doc.

SELECTION 7

The Bad Food and Drinks You Should Shun

Background

In "The Bad Food and Drinks You Should Shun," Muhammad highlighted the impact of pork on diminishing the thinking of people through the trichinae worm, which can travel to the brain. The selection detailed the impact of drinking and smoking on the reproductive organs as well as the overall health of people. Today, liquor and tobacco are marketed to Black youth through popular culture, which glamorizes their consumption. In their music videos, rap stars promote drinking and smoking, to the pleasure of those preying on Black youth.

Overview

One of the questions that Muslims are often confronted with is why they do not eat pork. In popular culture, such as movies and television shows, Black Muslims are often mocked because they do not eat pork. Elijah Muhammad taught that pork takes away the beautiful appearance of people. He also taught that the hog was not shy and that it was not meant to be eaten:

> God, in the Person of Master Fard Muhammad, taught me that the scientists have found that the hog carries 999 poisonous germs in it and they are not 100 percent poison, but nearly 1000 percent poison. The swine takes away our life gradually and creates worms in our bodies.

These worms, Muhammad explained, travel to the brain, which begins to impact the way one thinks and eventually leads to death. The trichinae worm, sometimes referred to as the "pork worm," cannot be seen with the naked eye but once consumed can lead to "other ailments such as fever, chills and headaches."

Elijah Muhammad was prescient in his discussion around food choices but also the impact of alcohol and tobacco on people. Today it is common to see videos of Black youth consuming liquor and smoking cigars. As a life-giving teacher, Elijah Muhammad said the following about alcoholic beverages:

> To drink whiskey, beer and wine when they have a high alcoholic content is against your and my health. These drinks have a tendency to be habit forming. When we become habitual drinkers, we are destroying our lives. If you want to live, you should not drink such beverages. You should not even drink a lot of soda pop. Some intelligent people will not drink one bottle of soda pop.

With regards to tobacco, he pointed out:

> If you want to live, stop smoking and chewing the poisonous weed (tobacco). Some of us are foolish enough to refer to our parents who chewed it and were 75 to 80 years old. That does not mean it was not harming them.

Any medical scientist will tell you that the tobacco weed is a very poisonous weed.

[...] Tobacco and alcoholic beverages also affect the organs of reproduction of young men. You should never use tobacco, whiskey, beer or wine. They ruin the reproductive organs and waste away the man power. Tobacco and alcoholic beverages also have this destructive effect upon the reproductive organs of women.

DISCUSSION QUESTIONS

In "The Bad Food and Drinks You Should Shun," the negative effects of eating pork and using tobacco and whiskey are discussed. Today marijuana is marketed to Black youth through popular culture.

1. In today's society, what are some of the ways this selection can help youth to become more conscious of how they are the targets of social engineering through the glorification of the use of drugs and intoxicating drinks?
2. How could you apply this reading in your own personal life?
3. What are three things that stood out to you in this selection?

TEST YOUR KNOWLEDGE

True or False?

1. Elijah Muhammad taught that pork did not affect the brain.
2. Popular culture images of Black youth do not include the consumption of liquor and tobacco.
3. Elijah Muhammad taught that highly intoxicating drinks affect the reproductive organs.
4. According to Elijah Muhammad, consuming soda on a daily basis will not have an impact on one's health.

REFERENCE

Muhammad, Elijah. (1967, July 7). "The bad food and drinks you should shun." *Muhammad Speaks*, 6(42).

SELECTION 8

Savagery of America

Background

In "Savagery of America," Muhammad discussed the decadent lifestyle of Americans and how in American society, there is no regard for human life. He likened the human being, the highest of God's creation, to beasts of the field. In modern America, the lives of human beings are snuffed out on a daily basis in contradiction to the teachings of the Holy Qur'an, which teaches that the killing of one person is like killing the whole of humanity. Today it's a compliment to be called *savage*.

Overview

In "Savagery of America," Elijah Muhammad disclosed what is today one of the biggest problems affecting America. This article was originally written in the 1970s, but it continues to be valuable as we have witnessed the devaluing of human life. Elijah Muhammad pointed out that despite all of America's advancement in knowledge, which has given birth to great innovations, the savagery displayed by its citizens is ever-increasing.

He attributed this type of behavior to the type of education people receive:

> The great and wonderful work of science on the earth and in the air, her great mighty fleets afloat on the high seas (on the surface and below the surface), her great scientific mechanical communications system! Yet with all of this might of skill in engineering or building, the country of America displays and practices more savagery than any civilized country on the earth. And all of her educational institutions are not enough to make a man so intelligent and proud of his education and of being an American citizen that he would not practice the same savagery.

His writings about murder, rape, and drug addiction in America can be easily observed by picking up a newspaper or turning on the television. From the murder of Black people to the hate crimes against Asians, America seems to be fulfilling what Muhammad wrote decades ago:

> It has become such a country that the civilized man of intelligence and decency is afraid to walk the streets of the vast towns and cities of America. He would be more secure in the jungles, around and in the midst of wild beasts than to be walking in the streets of these great cities in America after night.

DISCUSSION QUESTIONS

"Savagery of America" was written over 48 years ago, but it still speaks to the contemporary violence that is occurring in American society. Today, Black youth refer to themselves as *savage* and *beast*, in contrast to Elijah Muhammad's teachings that see the human being as the glory of God.

1. What does the violence in American society suggest about the education people are receiving in the 21st century?
2. How could this selection be applied in schools and universities in efforts to eradicate savagery?
3. What does this selection suggest about the need for new entertainment executives who promote a better image of human beings?
4. What are three things that stood out to you in this selection?

TEST YOUR KNOWLEDGE

True or False?

1. According to Elijah Muhammad, the savage behavior that is displayed across America is an indicator that something is deficient in the education of the American people.
2. Elijah Muhammad taught that people have a better chance of survival in the jungles than they do on the streets of America at night.
3. The education of people under the influence of Elijah Muhammad's teachings would address issues of civility.
4. Elijah Muhammad would be supportive of modern entertainment executives.

REFERENCE

Muhammad, Elijah. (1973). *The fall of America*. Secretarius MEMPS Publications.

SELECTION 9

He (Allah) Makes All Things New

Background

In "He (Allah) Makes All Things New," Muhammad disclosed knowledge of a future world. Modern advancements in technology and science now mirror what he taught about the emergence of a new world. This selection offered a new educational paradigm that counters the education that the masses experience. It demonstrated the many ways modern scientific and technological advancements have been fueled by Muhammad's teachings. A good example of this are his teachings about futuristic automobiles that would not use gas or pollute the air.

Overview

"He (Allah) Makes All Things New" was a forerunner to the technological world that we are now experiencing. Courses such as "Black Cyberspace" that are offered in Africana studies could be well served by infusing this selection into their readings. Elijah Muhammad's teachings have played a role in the technological innovations that are occurring.

His teachings in this selection disclose the creation of an entirely new universe. This would lead to a new heaven and new earth. He wrote that his teacher, Master Fard Muhammad, would "create a new heaven and a new earth, a new Islam and new government and people".

The new earth would come into existence after the final war, which would begin in America. After a thousand years of being consumed by the fire from that war, a new civilization would emerge, the likes of which has never been seen in human history. According to Elijah Muhammad, his teacher Master Fard Muhammad would not use anything in the present world to build this new world:

> This is the way of the Gods. One God is not allowed to pattern after another God when it comes to universal change. He is to use His own Wisdom. The white man brought about a universal change and so will Master Fard Muhammad, Allah, (God) in Person, bring about a new universal civilization. ...

He goes on to disclose the beginning of White rule and how long that rule was set to last:

> There was a new world of the white race that came into a vacuum in our history, from the 9,000th year to the 15,000th year of our calendar history, a vacuum made in our past 16,000 years, of 6,000 years, given to the white race to rule. We are now in the 15,000 year of our calendar history of 25,000 years.
>
> The rule of the white race terminates at the 16,000th year and that year is the beginning of the Black nation's rule again. ...

With regard to Islam, he wrote that its principles would remain the same but that there would be a new Islam that would emerge. The awakening of Blacks in America who had been lost to the knowledge of self would come first because they were at the bottom of the social ladder.

He used the analogy of how God created the heavens and earth from nothing, and so too would Master Fard Muhammad build a new people. The resurrection of the Blacks in America involves being exposed to a certain body of knowledge. Blacks in America can be likened to a sleeping lion that must be awakened to their greatness:

> As God created the present heaven and earth out of nothing, so will God, in the Person of Master Fard Muhammad, build a new heaven on earth from nothing (a people who are nothing) so that this world will have no claim on the making of the new people of the new heaven on earth.
>
> The Black man must be awakened to the knowledge of self—that he is not what the white race has taught him to be. ... He is to become the head of civilization of the new world or new heaven or earth. He is not to rule over this people, but he is to be the ruler of self, after the rule of the Caucasian, wicked world.

In his teachings about Islam, Elijah Muhammad spoke to the exclusiveness of a Black religion that is universal in scope. The freedom of Black people would be ushered in by God himself. Elijah Muhammad declared he was a messenger who was simply relaying a message he received from Master Fard Muhammad, God in person. His message included what the new world would look like:

> Allah (God) in the Person of Master Fard Muhammad, to Whom Praises are Due forever—out of His Own

Mouth—Said to me that He Causes us to Grow into a New Growth. And that we would have the look and the energy of one who is sixteen (16) years of age and our youth and energy of a sixteen-year-old would last forever.

In addition, Elijah Muhammad taught about what education in the new world would include. He envisioned first changing people's thought processes to introduce new ideas, as Allah makes all things new. The English language—that of the oppressors—wouldn't be spoken. Instead, a new language would be created. As God created new life, so could his followers birth new ideas and language.

Muhammad also mentioned the making of new automobiles that would not pollute the air and new forms of lighting that would not negatively impact the eye. The future envisioned in "He (Allah) Makes All Things New" has many similarities to the technological advancements we are currently experiencing.

DISCUSSION QUESTIONS

This selection, "He (Allah) Makes All Things New," is perhaps one of the most powerful writings of Elijah Muhammad. Embodied in this selection are ideas that have informed the modern, advanced world of technology and science. The selection even addresses *thought* and its impact on the physical appearance of people.

1. What are some of the ways this selection demonstrates similarities to the advancement of contemporary society?
2. What does Muhammad's discussion of the power of thought mean to you?
3. Briefly outline how this selection could be used to stimulate the creative minds of students.
4. What are three things that stood out to you in this selection?

TEST YOUR KNOWLEDGE

True or False?

1. According to Elijah Muhammad, a new world would come into existence after the final war.
2. According to Elijah Muhammad, Blacks in America would become the cornerstone of a new civilization.
3. In the new world Elijah Muhammad described, people would retain the appearance of a 16-year-old.
4. Elijah Muhammad believed that the resurrection of Blacks in America had nothing to do with knowledge.

REFERENCE

Muhammad, Elijah. (1974). *Our savior has arrived.* Secretarius MEMPS Publications.

About the Author

In this book, Abul Pitre, PhD, examines Elijah Muhammad's work within an educational context with the goal of making the reader aware of Muhammad's contribution to the disciplines of education and Africana studies. This book introduces readers to excerpts of selected writings, placed in a contemporary context.

The book pulls from Muhammad's classic works—*Message to the Blackman in America*, *Our Savior Has Arrived*, *The Fall of America*, and *How to Eat to Live*. Pitre situates Muhammad's work in a curriculum format for the reader to develop a program around the nine selections presented.

Each section begins with a short background to help the reader make connections to Elijah Muhammad's ideas for Black education. This is a must-read work for those interested in finding out how one of the most powerful men in history was able to transform the lives of countless people. Teachers and students in diverse disciplines will find this a welcome edition. Included in this book are discussion questions to stimulate critical thinking.

www.ingramcontent.com/pod-product-compliance
Lightning Source LLC
Chambersburg PA
CBHW070741230426
43669CB00014B/2537